Driveway Cookbook for the Football Season

A Deep Frying Cookbook

Written by:

John T. Guseman, *The Driveway Chef*

Thank you to the fans of the
Driveway Chef for faithfully
cheering me on and always
eating what comes out of my
fryer.

Thank you to Donna for showing
me I could do this project.

Thank you Nora and my family
for your never-ending support. I
will never be able to truly show
you the full extent of my
gratitude and love!

ISBN 13: 978-1-44-862314-3

ISBN: 1-44-862314-6

Introduction

Who is The Driveway Chef?

I am John T. Guseman, a guy who loves to fry in my garage, during football. Yes, it is quite exhilarating for me to cook food in the driveway as my friends, crazed football fans, cheer for our favorite team.

My frying frenzy started with my love for chicken wings and grew until I became an award winning fry chef with my own cookbook. It took a lot of experimentation. You name it, I've probably fried it. Turkey? Yes! Pizza? Yes! And yes, even that famous cream-filled yellow sponge cake!

For years now, I've tried to fry whatever I could think of with one special challenge in mind - to fry some food fitting for every single football team in the league. I did it, and this cookbook is the result. In its pages you will find my recipes to make mouth-watering fried favorites and some specialties you never even knew existed.

Whether you're looking for some creative frying recipes or a little humor to go with your fryer, your football, and your friends, *Driveway Chef's Cookbook for the Football Season* will expand your frying horizons.

Happy frying & enjoy the game,

John T. Guseman

The Driveway Chef

Table of Contents

Table of Contents

★★National★★

North

South

East

West

Getting Started

1. <u>Safety tips</u>
Always follow the safety guidelines that came with your fryer. Deep frying can become very dangerous very fast, so always be careful not to burn yourself or anything else.

2. <u>Types of oils</u>
I generally use peanut oil. I have found that it yields the best flavor. You can also use oils like vegetable oil, corn oil, canola oil, vegetable shortening, or safflower oil.

3. <u>Size of batches</u>
Most of these recipes yield 8 to 10 servings. Depending on your fryer, you probably will not be able to fry the entire recipe in one batch. Experiment with your own fryer to see how big of a batch of food you can fry at a time while maintaining the right temperature for frying.

4. <u>Flour based batters</u>
When batter involves flour, it may need slightly more or less flour than listed, depending on the type of flour being used. Keep in mind that the resulting batter should be similar to pancake batter. Mix as the recipe calls for, then adjust by adding flour or liquid as needed.

5. <u>Batters calling for beer</u>
I have tried all kinds of beer in beer batters. I have found that lighter beer makes a more crowd pleasing batter, but I encourage you to do your own experimentation.

6. <u>Temperature of oil</u>
I try to keep the oil in my fryer at about 365°F for the best frying results. When food goes into the oil, the temperature drops. Adjust the heat to maintain at least 350°F. The important thing is not to allow your oil to get above 400°F because most oils begin to smoke and break down around 400°F.

7. <u>Draining the food</u>
Most recipes call for draining before serving. My fryer allows me to drain the food right above the oil so the excess oil can go back into the fryer. In some cases, you might want to drain your food on paper towels before serving.

Pittsburg	Pickles
	Tomatoes
Cleveland	Hash Browns
	Corn Dogs
Baltimore	Potato Nest
	Raven Eggs
Cincinnati	Bengal Bites
	Carrot Cake

Pittsburgh

"Steel" yourself a great snack!

Pittsburgh Pickles
About 8 servings

2 cups flour
1 bottle (12 oz.) beer
1 teaspoon salt
24 pickle spears, well drained

Garnish: ketchup, mustard, bleu cheese dressing, teriyaki sauce

1. Mix flour, beer, and salt to form a batter.
2. Dip the pickles into the batter.
3. Deep fry for 2 minutes; then drain.
4. Serve on a steel plate.

Pittsburgh fans love their ketchup!

Deep Fried Tomatoes
About 8 servings

2 pounds large tomatoes
1 cup flour
4 eggs, beaten
2 cups seasoned bread crumbs

Garnish: ketchup

1. Slice all the tomatoes.
2. Roll in flour, dip in eggs, roll in bread crumbs.
   (Note: if they are not breaded enough put back in egg and re-roll in bread crumbs.)
3. Deep fry for 2 minutes; then drain.
4. Serve with ketchup, like you are in love.

Cleveland

Inspired by the colors of Cleveland

Hash "Browns"
About 8 servings

2 pounds shredded potatoes
1/4 cup chopped onions
2 eggs, beaten

Garnish: ketchup

1. Mix together the potatoes, onions, and eggs.
2. Take about 1/4 cup of mixture and make it into a patty. Repeat with remaining potato mixture.
3. Freeze the patties for at least 2 hours.
4. Deep fry the patties for 2 minutes, or until browned; then drain.
5. Garnish with ketchup, like you are inspired.

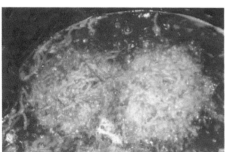

This one is for the dog pound.

Corn Dogs
About 8 servings

8 wooden skewers
8 hot dogs
1 cup pancake batter mix
1/2 cup corn meal
1 cup water

Garnish: ketchup or mustard

1. Skewer each hot dog lengthwise.
2. Mix the pancake mix, corn meal, and water into a batter.
3. Put the batter into a pint glass.
4. Dip the hotdogs into the batter.
5. Deep fry for 3 minutes; then drain.
6. Garnish like a dog!

Baltimore

A little something to put all your eggs in

Potato Nest
About 8 servings

2 pounds shredded potatoes

1. Deep fry in about one cup batches for about 2 minutes or until brown.
2. Drain and spread on a plate to use as a nest for the Raven Eggs (p. 11).

Best hatched idea!

Raven Eggs
About 8 servings

2 cups pancake mix
1 pound sausage cooked and drained
12 oz. water
1 cup flour
16 hard cooked eggs

Garnish: ketchup

1. Mix the pancake mix, sausage, and water to form a batter.
2. Roll the eggs in flour, then dip each egg into the batter.
3. Deep fry for 2 minutes or until golden brown; then drain.
4. Serve in the Potato Nest (p. 10).

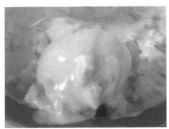

Cincinnati

Inspired by what makes Cincinnati exotic

Bengal Bites

About 8 servings

2 cans crescent roll dough (8 rolls each)
48 little cooked sausages

Garnish: ketchup and mustard

1. Cut each crescent roll into 3 small triangles.
2. Wrap each sausage in a crescent dough triangle.
3. Deep fry for 3 minutes or until dough is fully cooked; then drain.
4. Serve with ketchup and mustard, or exotic hot sauce.

The best orange striped food I've ever had.

Deep Fried Carrot Cake

About 8 servings

1 carrot cake
1 can (12 oz.) lemon-lime soda
2 cups flour
1 teaspoon sugar

Garnish: powdered sugar

1. Cut the carrot cake into wonderful slices.
2. Mix the soda, flour, and sugar to form a batter.
3. Dip each slice into the batter.
4. Deep fry for 2 minutes; then drain.
5. Tame with a sprinkle of powdered sugar.

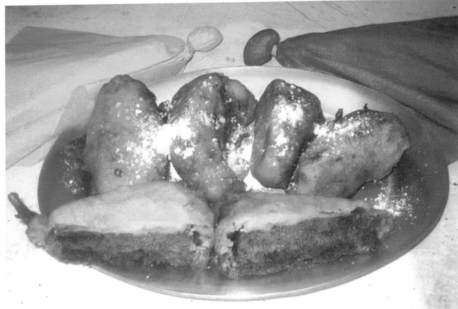

Indianapolis	**Macaroni and Cheese**
	Meat Loaf
Tennessee	**Catfish**
	Peanut Butter and Banana Sandwiches
Jacksonville	**Artichoke Hearts**
	Mushrooms, Cauliflower, Brussels Sprouts, and Zucchini
Houston	**Jalapeño Poppers**
	Texas Tots

Indianapolis

Everyone loves Midwestern comfort food!

Deep Fried Mac and Cheese
About 8 servings

2 boxes mac and cheese (about 7.25 oz. ea.)
4 eggs, beaten
1/2 cup water
1 cup flour
3 cups bread crumbs

1. Prepare the boxes of mac and cheese by following the directions on the box.
2. Flatten out the mac and cheese on a cookie sheet about 1 inch thick; then cool.
3. Mix the eggs and water together.
4. Cut mac and cheese into squares.
5. Roll each square in flour, dip in egg mixture, roll in bread crumbs.
   (Note: if they are not breaded enough put them back in egg and reroll in bread crumbs.)
6. Deep fry for 2 minutes; then drain.
7. Serve with great comfort.

For when you are as hungry as a horse

Deep Fried Meatloaf
About 8 servings

1 cooked meatloaf, 1-2 pounds (ask your mom for her recipe)
1 box of yeast bread mix

Garnish: ketchup or barbeque sauce

1. Refrigerate the meatloaf for at least 2 hours.
2. Slice the meatloaf in about 1/2-inch slices
3. Prepare the bread mix according to the box, but add a little more water to make it more like batter.
4. Dip the meatloaf slices into the batter.
5. Deep fry for about 2 minutes; then drain.
6. Garnish to your heart's content.

Tennessee

Every time I go to Tennessee I cannot get enough of these.

Catfish Nuggets
About 8 servings

2 pounds catfish
1 1/2 cups corn meal
1/2 cup flour
1 bottle (12 oz) beer
1/2 cup milk
1 teaspoon salt
2 tablespoons Cajun seasoning

Garnish: tartar sauce

1. Cut the catfish into nugget size pieces.
2. Mix the rest of the ingredients into a batter.
3. Batter each nugget
4. Deep fry for 5 minutes; then drain.
5. Garnish like you rule the world.

This one is for The King.

The King's Peanut and Banana Sandwich
About 8 servings

3 or 4 bananas
Creamy peanut butter
16 slices white bread
32 oz. cream soda
4 cups flour
2 teaspoons sugar

Garnish: powdered sugar.

1. Peel and smash the bananas.
2. Make 8 peanut butter and banana sandwiches.
3. Mix the soda, flour, and sugar to form a batter.
4. Dip the sandwiches into the batter.
5. Deep fry for 2 minutes, flipping half-way through; then drain.
6. Garnish like you are the king.

Jacksonville

Jaguar food

Deep Fried Artichoke Hearts with Parmesan Breading
About 8 servings

1 cup flour
3 eggs, beaten
1/4 cup water
1 cup seasoned bread crumbs
1/2 cup graded Parmesan cheese
3 cans (14 oz. ea.) artichoke hearts (or bottoms if you like), drained.

Garnish: ranch or bleu cheese dressing

1. Put the flour in a bowl
2. Mix the eggs and water together.
3. Combine the bread crumbs and cheese in a bowl.
4. Roll each artichoke in flour, dip in egg mixture, roll in bread crumbs.
    (Note: if they are not breaded enough put back in egg and reroll in bread crumbs.)
5. Deep fry for 2 minutes; then drain.
6. Don't "choke" as you garnish.

You'll be wild about these!

Deep Fried "Jungle" Veggies
About 8 servings

1/2 pound fresh mushrooms
1/2 pound cauliflower florets
1/2 pound zucchini
1/2 pound fresh Brussels sprouts
2 cups tempura batter mix
2 cups water
1 teaspoon salt

Garnish: ranch or bleu cheese dressing

1. Cut the vegetables as desired
2. Mix the tempura batter mix, water, and salt to form a batter.
3. Dip the vegetables into the batter.
4. Deep fry for 2 minutes; then drain.
5. Garnish like a jungle cat.

Houston

Inspired by the tastes of Texas

Jalapeño Poppers
About 8 servings

24 jalapeño peppers
1 can (8 oz.) pasteurized cheese snack
2 eggs, beaten
1/4 cup water
1 cup flour
2 cups bread crumbs

Garnish: ranch dressing for dip

1. Core the jalapeños.
2. Fill with cheese snack.
3. Mix eggs and water.
4. Roll each jalapeño pepper in flour, dip in egg mixture, roll in bread crumbs.
   (note: if they are not breaded enough put back in egg and reroll in bread crumbs.)
5. Deep fry for 2 minutes; then drain.
6. Garnish with a pop!

A flavor as big as the state of Texas

Texas Tots
About 8 servings

2 pounds frozen potato rounds
1 can(16 oz.) chili
1/2 pound shredded cheese

Garnish: sour cream, cayenne pepper hot sauce

1. Deep fry the potato rounds; then drain.
2. Cover with chili, and cheese.
3. If desired, microwave for 30 seconds to melt the cheese.
4. Garnish like a Texan.

New England	Musket Balls
	Fish and Chips
New York	Green Beans
	Jersey Street Dogs
Buffalo	Ice Cream Snow Balls
	Buffalo Wings
Miami	Chimichangas
	Rolled Tacos
	Plantains

New England

Something our forefathers might have used to fight off hunger

Musket Balls
About 8 servings

1 box sour dough bread mix
1 can (10.75 oz.) clam chowder soup

Garnish: hot sauce, ranch dressing, or cocktail sauce

1. Follow the directions for making the bread but use the clam chowder instead of water.
2. Roll the dough into balls about 3/4-inch in diameter. (Maybe use a little flour on your hands)
3. Deep fry the balls for 2 minutes or until fully cooked; then drain.
4. Garnish patriotically, or use as a topping for clam chowder.

New England

What was good for Old England is great for New England.

Fish and Chips
About 8 servings

2 cups flour
1 can (12 oz.) beer
1 teaspoon salt
5 pounds potatoes
2 pounds cod or other firm white fish

Garnish: tartar sauce, malt vinegar, cocktail sauce

1. Mix flour, beer, and salt to form a batter.
2. Cut the potatoes and fish into the size that you desire.
3. Batter the fish and deep fry for 3 minutes; then drain.
4. If the potato pieces are thin (about 1/4 in.), deep fry for 3 minutes or until golden brown; then drain.
5. If the potato pieces are thick, deep fry for 3 minutes, cool, then deep fry again for 3 minutes, or until golden brown; then drain.
6. Garnish like you are a red coat.

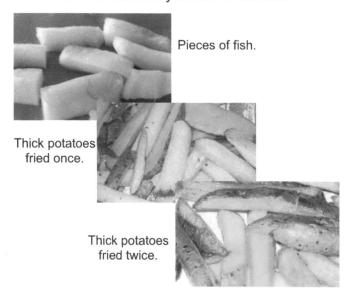

Pieces of fish.

Thick potatoes fried once.

Thick potatoes fried twice.

New York (American)

For those New Yorkers who root for the green team

Deep Fried Green Beans
About 8 servings

2 pounds green beans, trimmed
2 cups dry bread crumbs
2 eggs, beaten
1/2 cup water

Garnish: ranch dressing

1. Boil a pot of water, dip the green beans in boiling water for 1 minute; then drain.
2. Crush the bread crumbs with a rolling pin.
3. Mix the eggs and water.
4. Dip the green beans in the egg mixture, then roll them in the bread crumbs.
5. Deep fry for 1 minute; then drain.
6. Serve in a New York minute.

Breakfast on the street will never be the same.

Jersey Street Dog Special
About 8 servings

8 strips bacon
8 hotdogs
8 hotdog buns
16 slices American cheese.
8 eggs, fried

Garnish: ketchup or mustard

1. Wrap one strip of bacon around each hotdog, securing it with wooden picks.
2. Deep fry each bacon wrapped hotdog for 2 minutes; then drain and remove wooden picks.
3. Serve on a bun with 2 slices of cheese and a fried egg.
4. Garnish like you are streetwise.

Buffalo

Since it is so cold there

Ice Cream Snow Balls
About 8 servings

8 scoops ice cream
1 tablespoon ground cinnamon
1 cup granola
1 cup corn flakes, crushed down to 1/2 cup

Garnish: whipped cream, cinnamon, and Maraschino cherries.

1. Scoop the ice cream, then refreeze.
2. Mix the cinnamon, granola, and corn flakes into a coating.
3. Roll the ice cream in the mixture, then refreeze.
4. Deep fry each scoop for no more than 5 seconds, then drain.
5. Garnish like it's snowing.

Where it all started!

The Award Winning Buffalo Wings
About 8 servings

1/2 cup butter
1 cup cayenne pepper wing sauce
4 pounds chicken wings

Garnish: Cajun spice, sesame seed, carrots, celery, and bleu cheese dressing.

1. Melt the butter, mix with the cayenne pepper sauce.
2. Deep fry the wings for 6 minutes, or until internal temperature is above 160°F; then drain.
3. Roll the wings in the sauce.
4. Sprinkle with Cajun spice and sesame seed.
5. Garnish like you can fly!

Miami

These recipes are influenced by thoughts of Cuba.

Chimichangas
About 8 servings

2 cans (12 oz. ea.) refried beans
1 cup shredded cheese
16 flour tortillas (taco size)

Garnish: sour cream, salsa, lettuce, tomato, and additional cheese.

1. Scoop about 3 tablespoons of beans and about 1 tablespoon of cheese onto each tortilla.
2. Fold each tortilla and hold it together with two wooden picks.
3. Deep fry for 3 1/2 minutes; then drain.

How to fold a chimichanga:

Rolled Tacos (Taquitos)
About 8 servings

24 corn tortillas (taco size)
1 1/2 cups cooked shredded beef

Garnish: sour cream, salsa, lettuce, tomato, and cheese

1. Deep fry each tortilla for about 5 seconds; drain.
2. Spread about a tablespoon of shredded beef onto each tortilla.
3. Roll each tortilla and hold it together with a wooden pick.
4. Deep fry for 2 minutes; then drain.
5. Garnish like it's a fiesta!

Twice fried for double the impact

Fried Plantains
About 8 servings

6 plantains

   Garnish: salt, honey, or cinnamon and sugar

1. Peel the plantains. Sometimes it is easier to cut the peels off.
2. Cut into about 1/2 inch slices.
3. Deep fry for 3 minutes; then drain.
4. Flatten with the bottom of a beer bottle.
5. Deep fry again for 2 minutes; then drain.
6. Pick your favorite garnish and serve.

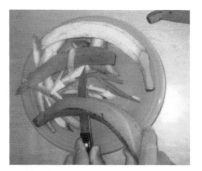

San Diego

Avocados

Tortilla Chips

Fish Tacos

Kansas City

Indian Fry Bread

Fried Chicken with
    Barbeque Sauce

Denver

Road Apples

Denver Omelet Turnover

Oakland

Sardines

Roots of Evil

San Diego

These recipes are inspired by the tastes of southern California

Fried Avocados

About 8 servings

1 bottle (12 oz.) favorite beer
2 cups flour
1 teaspoon salt
3 large avocados

Garnish: ranch dressing or salsa

1. Mix beer, flour and salt to form a batter.
2. Cut the avocados in half; discard pit.
3. Slice the avocados inside the skin.
4. Scoop the slices out with a spoon.
5. Dip the slices into the batter.
6. Deep fry for 3 minutes; then drain.

Tortilla Chips

*This is very easy and has a huge
"WOW" factor. Your friends will love these!*

About 8 servings

36 white or yellow corn tortillas
Salt or seasoned salt

Garnish: all of your favorite dips

1. Slice the tortillas into sixths.
2. Deep fry the pieces for 2 minutes, or until golden brown; then drain.
3. Sprinkle with salt or seasoned salt.
4. Dip away!

These will charge up any fiesta!

Fish Tacos
About 8 servings

2 lbs. tuna, mahi mahi, red snapper, or firm white fish
16 corn tortillas (taco size)
1/2 head green cabbage, shredded
1 bunch cilantro, chopped
2 limes cut into eighths

Garnish: cheese, guacamole, salsa, and sour cream

1. Cut the fish into medium sized strips.
2. Use batter from the Fried Avocadoes (p. 36).
3. Dip the fish into the batter.
4. Deep fry for 3 minutes or until golden brown; then drain.
5. Place 1 piece of fish on each tortilla along with cabbage, cilantro, and a squeeze of lime.
6. Garnish like it's a fiesta!

Kansas City

Any chief would love this!

Indian Fry Bread
About 8 servings

2 1/2 cups flour
2 teaspoons baking powder
1 teaspoon sugar
1 cup milk

Garnish: powdered sugar

1. Mix all the ingredients except the garnish in a bowl.
2. Take 1/4 to 1/2 cup of dough and flatten it out, like a thick tortilla.
3. Fry for 2 minutes, or until fully cooked, flipping half way through; then drain.
4. Sprinkle with powdered sugar, and get ready to pow wow.

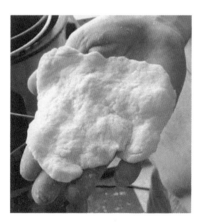

They love their barbeque sauce in Kansas City.

Fried Chicken with Barbeque Sauce
About 8 servings

4 pounds of chicken, cut into pieces
salt water (2 quarts water, 1 tablespoon salt)
4 cups flour
4 teaspoons pepper

Garnish: barbeque sauce

1. Soak the chicken for 2 hours in cold salt water; then drain and reserve remaining salt water.
2. Roll each piece of chicken in flour.
3. Dip chicken back into the salt water, bouncing it in a wire basket to create texture.
4. Re-roll breaded chicken in the flour.
5. Fry the chicken for about 6 minutes, or until it is fully cooked; then drain.
6. Serve with barbeque sauce.

Denver

Think of them as little gifts for you from your favorite horse.

Road Apples
About 8 servings

4 apples, cored and quartered
1 cup caramel sauce
1 cup coconut shavings
1 cup chopped nuts
16 large wonton wrappers

Garnish: caramel sauce

1. Coat each apple quarter with caramel sauce
2. Roll in coconut shavings and chopped nuts.
3. Wrap each apple in a wonton wrapper, sealing with a dab of water.
4. Deep fry for 2 minutes; then drain.
5. Scoop up with a little garnish.

I could not pass on this one!

Denver Omelet Turnover

About 8 servings

6 eggs, beaten
1/4 cup milk
1/4 cup diced ham
1/4 cup diced onion
1/4 cup diced green pepper
1/4 cup shredded cheese
2 cans refrigerated crescent rolls (8 rolls each)
Salt and pepper

Garnish: ketchup or salsa

1. Mix eggs, milk, ham, onion, green pepper, and cheese in a bowl.
2. Scramble the egg mixture in a pan until cooked.
3. Unroll the crescent dough into triangles.
4. Scoop about 2 tablespoons egg mixture onto one triangle.
5. Place another triangle on top and seal with a fork.
6. Deep fry each turnover for 2 minutes (or until done), turning half way through; then drain.
7. Hand them off to be garnished.

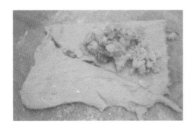

Oakland

An homage to Oakland fans everywhere

Deep Fried Silver and Black
About 8 servings

4 small cans sardines in oil
1 1/2 cups corn meal
1 cup flour
1 bottle (12 oz.) beer
1 teaspoon black food coloring
1 teaspoon salt

Garnish: mustard

1. Roll the sardines in 1 cup cornmeal.
2. Mix the rest of the ingredients, except garnish, into a batter.
3. Dip each sardine into the batter and fry for 2 minutes, then drain.
4. Garnish like you are in a black hole.

A great snack when you are feeling a little evil

The Roots of Evil Chips
About 8 servings

1/2 pound of taro root
1/2 pound of beets
1/2 pound of sweet potatoes
1/2 pound of russet potatoes
salt water

Garnish: your favorite dip

1. Slice all the roots, extremely thin. (I know a potato is actually a tuber, but it fits the theme)
2. Soak all the slices in salt water for at least 30 minutes; then drain.
3. Deep fry for 3 minutes; then drain.

Chicago	Hotdog
	Pizza
Green Bay	Cheese Curds
	Bratwurst
Detroit	French Fries
	Lion Balls
Minnesota	Cream Filled Sponge Cake
	Beef Nuggets

Chicago

Good old-fashioned Chicago eats with a frying twist

Chicago Style Hot Dog
About 8 servings

8 all-beef hot dogs
8 poppy seed buns

Garnish: Sweet pickle relish, red tomato wedges, pickle wedges, chopped white onion,
       celery salt, mustard, sport or poblano peppers

Steps
1. Wrap 2 or 3 hot dogs at a time in foil.
2. Deep fry the foil wrapped dogs for 3 minutes; then drain.
3. "Steam" the buns on a rack over the deep fryer while frying something else.
4. Garnish like nobody's business!

It is worth coming out of hibernation for this!

Deep Fried Pizza
About 8 servings

1 1/2 cup cornmeal
1 1/2 cups flour (divided)
1 bottle (12 oz.) beer
1/2 cup milk
1 teaspoon salt
2 medium leftover pizzas, refrigerated

Garnish: parsley and marinara

1. Mix cornmeal, 3/4 cup flour, beer, milk and salt to form a batter.
2. Dip each pizza slice in the remaining flour; gently shake off excess flour.
3. Dip each pizza slice in the cornmeal batter.
4. Deep fry for 2 minutes, turning each slice after 1 minute; then drain.
5. Cut each slice in half then garnish like you own a pizzeria. (Serving in a box is a fun touch.)

Green Bay

When I am in Green Bay, these are a must!

Deep Fried Cheese Curds
About 8 servings

2 pounds fresh cheese curds
2 eggs, beaten
1 cup flour
2 cups seasoned bread crumbs

Garnish: marinara sauce

1. Roll the curds in flour, dip in eggs, roll in bread crumbs.
   (Note: if they are not breaded enough put back in egg and re-roll in bread crumbs.)
2. Deep fry for 1 minute, or until the cheese starts to ooze out; then drain.
3. Dip in the sauce don't cha know!

Green Bay

Beer and brats go together like yellow and green!

Beer Bratwurst
About 8 servings

8 bratwurst, fully cooked
8 buns
3 bottles (12 oz. ea.) beer

Garnish: mustard, sauerkraut, diced onions, pickles, crumbs

1. Deep fry the bratwurst for 4 minutes; then drain.
2. Boil them in beer until you are ready to eat.
3. Place in bun and garnish like a meat packer.

Detroit

A side dish for the king of the jungle

French Fries
About 8 servings

2 pounds of potatoes, cleaned

Garnish: ketchup and salt

1. Cut the potatoes into about 1/4 strips. (A mandolin makes this easy.)
2. Deep fry for 3 minutes, or until crispy brown; then drain.
3. Sprinkle with salt and serve with ketchup along side your favorite dish.

The tastiest thing that might bite back

Lion Balls
About 8 servings

2 pounds ground beef
1 cup shredded cheese
1 cup dill relish
1 box bread mix

Garnish: ketchup

1. Mix ground beef, cheese, and dill relish in a large bowl.
2. Scoop 2 or 3 tablespoons of the mixture and roll into a ball. Repeat with remaining mixture.
3. Mix the bread dough according to the directions on the box, but thin it with a little water to make it a batter.
4. Dip each ball into the batter.
5. Deep fry for 3 minutes; then drain.
6. Garnish with a roar.

Minnesota

This one goes out to the twin cities!

Deep Fried Cream Filled Yellow Sponge Cake
About 8 servings

1 can (12 oz.) lemon lime soda
2 cups flour
1 teaspoon sugar
16 cream filled yellow sponge cakes

Garnish: blueberry pie filling and powdered sugar

1. Mix soda, flour, and sugar to form a batter.
2. Dip each cream filled yellow sponge cake into the batter.
3. Deep fry for 2 minutes; then drain.
4. Garnish twice.

For those Vikings with a carnivorous reputation

Beef Nuggets

About 8 servings

2 pounds beef sirloin steak
2 tablespoons mustard
1 tablespoon steak sauce

Garnish: your favorite dipping sauces

1. Trim and cube the beef.
2. Deep fry the cubes for 45 seconds (or until fully cooked); then drain.
3. Mix the mustard and steak sauce for a dipping sauce.
4. Garnish with lakes of your favorite dipping sauces.

New Orleans	Angel Food Cake
	Monte Crispos
Atlanta	Peach Turnover
	Cola Cherries
Carolina	Okra
	Hush Puppies
Tampa Bay	Fish Sticks
	Shrimp

New Orleans

A heavenly food for any saint

Deep Fried Angel Food Cake
About 8 servings

1 cup pecans
30 vanilla wafer cookies
1 egg
1/4 cup caramel sauce
3/4 cup water
1 angel food cake

Garnish: caramel and powdered sugar

1. Put pecans and cookies into a food processor and pulse until fine crumbs form.
2. Combine crumbs, egg, caramel sauce and water; mix well to form a batter.
3. Slice the angel food cake and dip into the batter.
4. Deep fry for 2 minutes, turning after 1 minute; then drain.
5. Garnish like you are in the Big Easy.

Cookie and nut crumbs

Garnished with caramel and powdered sugar

A French delight with a crispy twist

Monte Crispos
About 8 servings

frozen French toast sticks
1/4 lb. sliced ham
1/4 lb. gouda cheese

12 oz Champagne
2 cups flour
1 teaspoon salt

Garnish: jelly or jam

1. Cut a slit lengthwise in each French toast stick.
2. Slice the ham, then cut into 1/2 inch strips.
3. Slice the gouda into 1/4-inch thick slices.
4. Fill each French toast stick with slices of ham and gouda.
5. Mix the Champagne, flour, and salt to form a batter.
6. Dip each stick into the batter.
7. Deep fry for 2 minutes; then drain.
8. Garnish like you are in the French Quarter.

Atlanta

Can't beat those Georgia peaches!

Peach Turnover
About 8 servings

2 cans crescent roll dough (8 rolls ea.)
1 can (21 oz.) peach pie filling

Garnish: powdered sugar

1. Unroll the crescent dough into triangles.
2. Place 2 or 3 peach slices and a spoonful of pie filling on each triangle.
3. Place another triangle on top and seal with a fork.
4. Deep fry each turnover for 3 minutes (or until done), turning half way through; then drain.
5. Serve with southern hospitality.

A hot twist on Atlanta's favorite cold drink

Deep Fried Cola Cherries
About 8 servings

8 oz. cola
1 cup flour
1/2 teaspoon sugar
2 jars (10 oz. ea.) Maraschino cherries with stems (40 cherries), drained.

Garnish: chocolate syrup

<u>Steps</u>
1. Mix the cola, flour, and sugar to form a batter.
2. Dip each cherry into the batter.
3. Deep fry for 1 minute or until golden brown; then drain.
4. Drizzle with chocolate syrup.

Carolina

Good old-fashioned southern food.

Deep Fried Okra
About 8 servings

2 eggs, beaten
1 cup flour
2 cups seasoned bread crumbs
2 pounds of cut okra

Garnish: ranch dressing

1. Roll the okra in flour, dip in eggs, roll in bread crumbs.
   (Note: if they are not breaded enough put back in egg and re-roll in bread crumbs.)
2. Deep fry for 2 minutes; then drain.
3. Dip like you are down on the plantation!

These will hush a few hungry panthers as well.

Hush Puppies
About 8 servings

1 1/2 cups corn meal
1 1/2 cups flour
1 tablespoon sugar
1 teaspoon baking powder
1 teaspoon baking soda
1 teaspoon salt
1 teaspoon pepper (optional)
1 cup buttermilk
2 eggs, beaten

Garnish: honey

1. Mix all the ingredients, except honey, into a batter.
2. Scoop about 1/4 cup of batter and roll into a ball. (Flour on your hands might help.)
3. Deep fry for 5 minutes or until fully cooked; then drain.
4. Serve with honey and a southern drawl.

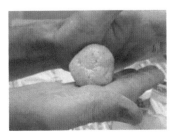

Tampa Bay

Gotta love seafood in the bay!

Fish Sticks
About 8 servings

2 pounds cod or white fish
1 bottle (12 oz.) beer
2 cups flour
1 teaspoon salt

Garnish: tartar sauce

1. Cut the fish into 1/2-inch thick sticks.
2. Mix the beer, flour, and salt into a batter.
3. Dip the fish into the batter.
4. Deep fry for 4 minutes, or until fully cooked; then drain.
5. Garnish like a swashbuckler.

You might be willing to walk the plank for these.

Deep Fried Shrimp
About 8 servings

4 eggs, beaten
1 cup flour
2 cups Italian style panko breadcrumbs
2 pounds of large cooked and peeled shrimp

Garnish: cocktail sauce

1. Roll shrimp in flour, dip in eggs, roll in bread crumbs.
   (Note: if they are not breaded enough put back in eggs and re-roll in bread crumbs.)
2. Deep fry for 2 minutes; then drain.
3. Dip away, matey!

Philadelphia   **Pretzels**

                              Cheesesteak Footballs

New York   **Cheesecake**

                              Spaghetti

Dallas   **Stuffing**

                              Mashed Potatoes in Gravy Batter

                              Turkey

Washington   **Potato Skins**

                              Red Pepper Poppers

Philadelphia

Inspired by pretzel fans of the world

Pretzels
About 8 servings

1 box pizza dough mix

Garnish: coarse salt, mustard

1. Make the pizza dough according to the directions on the box.
2. Roll 1- 2 tablespoons of dough on a floured board into a log about 14-16 inches long.
3. Fold into pretzel shape; repeat with remaining dough.
4. Deep fry for 2 minutes, drain, and sprinkle with coarse salt.
   (If the salt does not stick, rub a little water on top of the pretzel and re-sprinkle.)
5. Serve with mustard, if you must.

Philadelphia

A spin on the food that made Philadelphia famous.

Cheesesteak Footballs, *"Wit"* (with grilled onions)
About 10 servings

5 frozen, thinly sliced, uncooked sandwich steaks
2 cans refrigerated biscuits (10 biscuits ea.)
1 large onion, diced and sautéed
1 can (8 oz.) pasteurized cheese snack

Garnish: more cheese!

1. Cook the steaks according to package directions, then chop and separate into 10 portions.
2. Separate each biscuit into two pieces and flatten into an oval about 4 inches long.
3. Fill each with one portion of steak, about 2 teaspoons of onion, and 1 good squirt of cheese.
4. Top with the second oval and shape like a football. Pinch along the edge to seal.
5. Deep fry for 3 minutes or until golden brown, flipping half way through; then drain.
6. Garnish like you have a mullet.

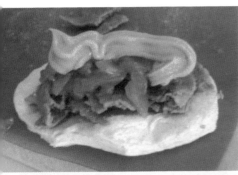

New York (National)

The newest New York style dessert.

Deep Fried New York Style Cheesecake
About 8 servings

1 New York style cheesecake
2 packages of large wonton wrappers

Garnish: whipped cream, cherry pie filling, and chocolate sauce

1. Cut the cheese cake into thin slices.
2. Wrap each slice with a wonton wrapper.
3. Deep fry for 1 1/2 minutes; then drain.
4. Garnish like you are in the Big Apple.

What New Yorker wouldn't like this spaghetti?

Deep Fried Spaghetti in Garlic Batter

About 8 servings

2 pounds spaghetti, cooked
2 cups spaghetti sauce
1 box yeast bread mix
1 teaspoon garlic powder
1 teaspoon garlic salt
water

Garnish: marinara sauce for dipping

1. Mix the spaghetti and sauce in a bowl.
2. Scoop about 1/4 cup into each hole of a muffin tin; then freeze at least 2 hours.
3. Mix the bread mix according to package directions, adding garlic powder and garlic salt.
4. Add water as needed to thin to batter consistency.
5. Dip each spaghetti "muffin" into the batter.
6. Deep fry for 3 minutes; then drain.
7. Serve with marinara and dip like you are in the mob.

Dallas

These recipes are in the spirit of Thanksgiving.

Deep Fried Stuffing
About 10 servings

1 box (12 oz.) stuffing mix
1 cup chopped celery
1 cup chopped onion
1/2 cup melted butter
6 eggs, beaten

Garnish: gravy

1. Mix all ingredients, except gravy, in a bowl.
2. Form stuffing into patties.
3. Deep fry for 2 minutes; then drain.
4. Serve thankfully.

Deep Fried Mashed Potatoes in Gravy Batter
About 10 servings

5 cups mashed potatoes
1 cup gravy
1/4 cup flour

1. Scoop the mashed potatoes onto a cookie sheet and put into the freezer for about an hour. (You do not want to freeze them completely, just firm enough to batter them.)
2. Mix gravy and flour. (You may need more or less flour depending on the thickness of your gravy to make a batter.)
3. Dip the mashed potatoes into the batter.
4. Deep fry for 3 minutes; then drain.

Cowboys and city slickers alike love this turkey.

Deep Fried Turkey

Always be safe! Wear heat proof gloves and protective eye wear. Most turkey fryers come with full safety instructions. Please follow them. Do not burn yourself or your house down.

1. **Figure out oil level** - Place the turkey inside the empty pot. Fill the pot with cold water until it is about 1 inch above the turkey. (For safety, this level should be no more than 2/3 to the top of the pot.) Lift, drain, and pat dry the turkey. The remaining water level will be how much oil is needed to fry the turkey. Remove the water and dry the fryer.

2. **Prior to frying** - Multiply the weight of the turkey by 3.5, this will be your frying time in minutes. For example, a 16 pound turkey will take about 56 minutes. Find a safe place, away from anything flammable to fry the turkey. Make sure the turkey and pot are dry. Fill the pot with oil to the predetermined level and preheat to 365°F.

3. **Frying** - Once the oil is heated to 365°F, SLOWLY lower your turkey into the oil. Once the turkey is fully submerged put on a splatter guard, start the timer, and monitor the temperature of the oil; try to keep the oil between 325°F and 350°F.

4. **After Frying** - Slowly lift up the turkey and make sure that the internal temperature is above 165°F. Let it fully drain. Carve, serve, and be thankful!

Washington

A popular snack, even better deep fried!

Red Skins
About 8 servings

10 lbs. red potatoes
4 cups shredded cheddar cheese

Garnish: sour cream, crumbed cooked bacon, chives, ketchup, ranch dressing, salsa.

1. Pierce the skins of the potatoes with a fork. Bake at 400°F for 40 minutes or until they can be pierced easily with a fork. Cool.
2. Cut each potato in half and hollow out with a spoon.
3. Deep fry the potato halves for 3 minutes or until golden; then drain.
4. Serve with ketchup, ranch dressing, or salsa.
5. Garnish in a capital fashion!

Another red-skinned food to enjoy

Red Pepper Poppers

About 8 servings

4 red bell peppers
2 cups shredded Monterey Jack cheese
1 package (6 oz.) goat cheese

2 cups flour
1 bottle (12oz.) beer
1 teaspoon salt

Garnish: salt and pepper

1. Remove stems, cores, and seeds of each red pepper and cut into pieces.
2. Mix cheeses in a small bowl.
3. Scoop about 1 tablespoon of the cheese mixture into each red pepper piece.
4. Mix flour, beer, and salt to form a batter.
5. Dip each filled red pepper piece in the batter.
6. Deep fry for 2 minutes or until golden; then drain.
7. Tastes best when cut open and sprinkled with salt and pepper.

Arizona	Candy Bars and Cookies
	Apples
San Francisco	Golden Nuggets
	Egg Rolls
St. Louis	Onion Arches
	Ravioli
Seattle	Rice Nest
	Cornish Game Hens
All Pro Game	Spiced Ham
	Pineapple

Arizona

There is nothing better to eat in the desert than dessert.

Fried Candy Bars and Cookies
About 8 servings

1 can (12 oz.) lemon-lime soda
2 cups flour
1 teaspoon sugar
1 pound bag of small candy bars
1 pound container of chocolate cream sandwich cookies

Garnish: powered sugar

1. Mix the soda, flour, and sugar to form a batter.
2. Dip each bar and cookie into the batter.
3. Deep fry for 2 minutes; then drain.
4. Garnish generously.

Red delicious indeed!

Fried Apples
About 8 servings

4 Red Delicious apples

Garnish: caramel sauce, cinnamon, whipped cream, powdered sugar, and ice cream.

1. Slice the apples in your favorite way.
2. Deep fry them for 2 minutes; then drain.
3. Let your sweet tooth do the garnishing.

San Francisco

Inspired by what put this place on the map

Gold Rush Nuggets
About 8 servings

2 pounds fresh boneless, skinless chicken breast
2 quarts salt water (2 quarts of water and 1 tablespoon salt)

Batter
2 cups flour
1 bottle of beer
1/4 cup water
1 teaspoon seasoned salt
1 teaspoon pepper or your favorite seasoning

Garnish: barbeque sauce, mustard, ketchup

1. Cut the chicken in nugget size pieces.
2. Soak the chicken pieces in cold salt water for 30 minutes.
3. Mix the ingredients for the batter in a bowl.
4. Drain the chicken; pat it dry.
5. Dip the chicken pieces into the batter.
6. Deep fry for 3 minutes; then drain.
7. Garnish like you are striking it rich!

San Francisco

Another favorite food of the football fans of the region

Chicken Egg Rolls
About 8 servings

12 oz. cooked, shredded chicken
12 oz. chopped coleslaw mix
4 oz. bean sprouts
2 oz. canned mushrooms, drained and finely chopped
1 oz. water chestnuts, finely chopped
2 teaspoon soy sauce
1 teaspoon curry powder
16 large wonton wrappers

Garnish: mustard and soy sauce

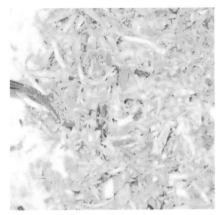

Egg roll filling

1. Mix all the ingredients except the wonton wrappers and garnish in a large bowl .
2. Scoop about 1/4 cup of filling onto each wonton wrapper.
3. Fold up one corner, then fold up the sides.
4. Roll up and seal the last corner with a little dab of water.
5. Deep fry for about 2 minutes, or until golden brown.
6. Garnish like you just went to China-town.

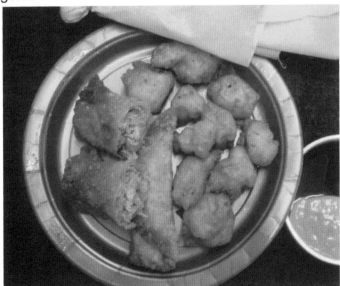

St. Louis

A landmark recipe

Ram Rings and St. Louis Arches
About 8 servings

1 bottle (12 oz.) beer
2 cups of flour
1 teaspoon salt
2 large yellow onions

Garnish: ketchup, mustard or ranch dressing

1. Mix the beer, flour, and salt to form a batter.
2. Slice the onions into about 1/2-inch slices.
3. For Ram Rings, cut the larger rings and spiral them on a skewer.
4. For St. Louis arches, cut the smaller rings into arches.
5. Batter the Ram Rings and St. Louis Arches.
6. Deep fry for 3 minutes, or until golden; then drain.

For the batter, it might be helpful to sift the flour first.

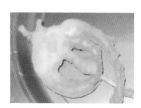

Ram Rings

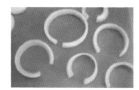

St. Louis Arches

A gateway food!

Fried Ravioli
About 8 servings

2 pounds ravioli, cooked

Garnish: marinara sauce

1. Deep fry cooked ravioli for 2-3 minutes depending on the size of your ravioli, stirring often; then drain.
2. Garnish in a saintly fashion.

Seattle

There is no better food for a game hawk to rest on.

Wild Rice Hawk's Nests
About 8 servings

3 cups cooked wild rice
3 eggs, beaten
3/4 cup dry bread crumbs
3/4 cup shredded cheese
3/4 cup breakfast sausage, cooked and crumbled

1. Mix all ingredients in a medium bowl.
2. Form the mixture into 8 patties and place onto a cookie sheet. Press with a spoon to make a nest shape.
3. Freeze for at least one hour.
4. Deep fry each for about 2 minutes, then drain.
5. Save as the nest for your Cornish Game Hawk (p.83).

A "nest" before going into the freezer.

You may want to vary the size of your "nests"

For everyone who wants a little of that Hawk by the sea

Cornish Game Hawks

About 8 servings

4 Cornish game hens, fresh or thawed

Garnish: rosemary and ketchup

1. Calculate the frying time for your hens based on about 3.5 minutes per pound.
2. Deep fry game hens for the calculated time, or until internal temperature is 165°F; then drain.
3. Place on a cooked Wild Rice Hawk's Nest (p. 82) and garnish wildly.

Make sure to check that the internal temperature is at lest 165°F.

All Pro Game

A Hawaiian favorite

Fried Spiced Ham and Macaroni Salad
About 8 servings

2 cans (12 oz.) spiced ham
1 large tub macaroni salad

Garnish: hot sauce, pepper

1. Slice the ham into about 1/4-inch slices.
2. Deep fry the slices for 4 minutes; then drain.
3. Sprinkle with hot sauce, pepper and serve with a big ol' tub of macaroni salad.

All Pro Game

This one is inspired by the big Hawaiian game.

Deep Fried Pineapples
About 8 servings

1 can (12 oz.) lemon-lime soda
2 cups flour
1 teaspoon sugar
2 cans (20 oz. ea.) sliced pineapples, drained and patted dry

Garnish: powdered sugar

1. Mix the soda, flour, and sugar to form a batter.
2. Dip the pineapple slices into the batter.
3. Deep fry for 2 minutes, turning after 1 minute; then drain.
4. Sprinkle with powdered sugar, and serve like you are the best of the best!

Index of Recipes

Index of Teams

Index of Teams

Made in the USA